SPACE UNIVERSITY™

# THE SPACE EXPLORER'S GUIDE TO

# the Search for Life in the Universe

BY
## BILL DOYLE

WITH **RACHEL CONNOLLY**
SPACE EDUCATOR

**RYAN WYATT**
VISUAL ADVISOR

AND **JIM SWEITZER**, PH.D.
NASA SCIENCE CENTER,
DePaul University

SCHOLASTIC INC.

NEW YORK   TORONTO   LONDON   AUCKLAND   SYDNEY
MEXICO CITY   NEW DELHI   HONG KONG   BUENOS AIRES

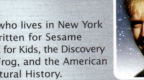
# Who's Who at Space U

## Bill Doyle
### Writer

Bill is a writer who lives in New York City. He has written for Sesame Workshop, TIME for Kids, the Discovery Channel, LeapFrog, and the American Museum of Natural History.

## Rachel Connolly
### Consultant

Rachel manages the astrophysics education program at the American Museum of Natural History's Rose Center for Earth and Space.

## Ryan Wyatt
### Visual Advisor

Ryan designs scientific visuals for the American Museum of Natural History's Rose Center for Earth and Space.

## Jim Sweitzer
### Advisor

Jim is an astrophysicist and the director of the NASA Space Science Center at DePaul University in Chicago.

ISBN: 0-439-55742-9

Copyright © 2004 by Scholastic Inc.

Editor: Andrea Menotti
Assistant Editor: Megan Gendell
Designers: Peggy Gardner, Lee Kaplan, Tricia Kleinot, Robert Rath
Illustrators: Daniel Aycock, Yancey C. Labat, Thomas Nakid, Ed Shems

Photos:
Front cover: A spiral galaxy that's about 60 million light years away from Earth
(image by the Hubble Heritage Team—AURA/STScI/NASA).
Back cover: One of the *Voyager* probes passing Jupiter's moon Europa (images by NASA/JPL).
Title page: The Very Large Array, a big group of radio telescopes in New Mexico (image by David Nunuk/Photo Researchers).
Page 7: Dr. Tim Evans/Photo Researchers. Page 8: (water) Adam Hart-Davis/Photo Researchers.
Page 10: (Mars) NASA/STScI/Colorado/Cornell/SSI, (Mars landscape) NASA/JPL. Page 12: (A and D) Andrew Syred/Photo
Researchers, (B and E) Eye of Science/Photo Researchers, (C) Microfield Scientific Ltd./Photo Researchers.
Page 13: (hot springs) Bonnie Sue Rauch/Photo Researchers, (rock-eating bacteria) T. Stevens & P. McKinley, PNNL/Photo
Researchers, (desert varnish) Andrea Menotti. Page 14: (snow algae) Benjamin Drummond, (Moon) NASA/JPL/USGS.
Page 15: OAR/National Undersea Research Program/NOAA. Page 17 (black smoker): B. Murton/Southampton Oceanography
Centre/Photo Researchers, (Europa) NASA/DLR, (close-up) NASA/U.S. Geological Survey. Page 19: courtesy of Lynn Rothschild.
Page 31: NRAO/AUI. Page 32 (Frank Drake) and page 33 (Dr. Kent Cullers): Seth Shostak, SETI Institute.
Page 33: (radio telescopes) NRAO/AUI. Page 35, top: NASA. Page 38, top: NASA. Page 38, bottom: (Voyager) NASA/JPL.
Page 38, 42, and 44: (Golden Record surface) NASA. Page 39, top: NASA. Page 44, left: courtesy of Ann Druyan.
Page 45, bottom: Mary Evans Picture Library. Page 46, bottom: Bettmann/Corbis. Page 48, bottom: NASA.

12 11 10 9 8 7 6 5 4 3 2                                        4 5 6 7 8/0

Printed in the U.S.A.

First Scholastic printing, January 2004

The publisher has made every effort to ensure that the activities in this book are safe when done as instructed.
Adults should provide guidance and supervision whenever the activity requires.

# Table of **Contents**

**Hello...Is Anyone Out There?** ............................................... 4
   What's in This Month's Space Case? ....... 6
   This Month's Space University Web Site
      and Planet Password ........................ 6

**Part 1: What *Is* Life, Anyway?** ............................. 7
   What Does Life Need? ............................................. 8
   Mission: Create Your Own Life Detector! ................. 9
   Mission: Mold on Hold ........................................... 11
   The "X" Files ........................................................... 13
   Where There's Smoke... ........................................ 15
   Mission: Up in Smoke! ............................................ 16
   Astrobiology ........................................................... 18
   Meet the Stars: Astrobiologist Dr. Lynn Rothschild ....... 19

**Part 2: Make Your Own Aliens** ............... 20
   The Stellar Six-Planet Tour .................................... 21
   Planet Machisimus ................................................. 22
   Planet Glubinsploosh .............................................. 23
   Planet Airupthere .................................................. 24
   Planet Pthurst ....................................................... 25
   Planet Hotstuff ...................................................... 26
   Planet Seerogee ..................................................... 27
   Life Is What You Make It! ....................................... 28

**Part 3: Searching for Intelligent Life** ................... 31
   Meet the Stars: SETI Scientist Dr. Kent Cullers ........... 33
   Wave Hello! ............................................................ 34
   Alien Math Test ..................................................... 35
   Mission: Alien Code ............................................... 36
   From Earth with Love ............................................ 38
   Earth's Greatest Hits! ........................................... 39
   Greetings from Earth ............................................ 40
   The Sounds of Earth .............................................. 42
   Meet the Stars: Golden Record Creative Director Ann Druyan ....... 44

**Part 4: Past Mysteries and Future Possibilities** .......... 45
   Maybe, Someday... ............................................... 47

**Life Goes On!** ......................................................... 48
   The Answer Station ............................................... 48

# HELLO...

For centuries, curious minds like yours have wondered, "Are there alien creatures somewhere in the universe just waiting to be discovered?"

In this next step in your Space University training, we'll help you search for these *extraterrestrials*, otherwise known as ETs. We'll give you the tools you need to investigate questions like:

An **extraterrestrial (ET)** is a living being that makes its home somewhere other than Earth.

- What *is* life—and what wild and wacky forms can it take here on Earth?

- Is there life—green or otherwise—on Mars?

- Are there ETs on the Moon?

- What would an ET look like if it lived on a planet filled with fire? On a planet made of ice?

- Where and how are we searching for life in the universe right now?

- Could an ET across the galaxy someday watch your favorite TV show?

- If there *is* intelligent life out there, how can we make contact?

An alien! Cool!

An alien! Cool!

# Is Anyone Out There?

### HOW CAN I TRACK DOWN ALIEN LIFE?

There are possibly billions and billions of planets in the universe—so where should you launch your quest for ETs?

In this book, you'll start your search for life right here on Earth, then travel to Mars and one of Jupiter's moons. Finally, you'll blast out of the solar system to take a stellar six-planet tour. Each of the pretend planets on this tour could host all kinds of strange creatures—and *you* get to create them with the alien parts in this month's Space Case! By imagining all these out-of-this-world life forms, your brain will be totally prepped for your search for *real* life in the universe!

### AND WHAT MIGHT I FIND?

Of course, we have no idea what aliens might look like—or if we'll even be able to see them at all. Our own planet is covered with tiny forms of life called *microbes*, creatures we can't see without a microscope (like bacteria). Microbes were the only living creatures on our planet for most of its history, so scientists think that this is the kind of life we're most likely to find on another planet.

### BUT WHAT ABOUT INTELLIGENT LIFE?

Finding a microscopic ET is one thing, but finding a whole alien civilization with advanced technology, that's quite another!

"Intelligent life" is the way we describe any ET that has developed to the point that it can communicate with Earthlings. We like to think of ourselves as intelligent, after all—but who knows what our cosmic neighbors might think of us!

To search for intelligent life, scientists scan the sky for signals from distant civilizations, and we send out some of our own messages, too. See Part 3 of this book (starting on page 31) for more on this!

So, cadet, grab your Space Case, rev up your imagination, and get ready for another eye-opening month at Space U. See if it changes your *outlook* on life!

## WHAT'S IN THIS MONTH'S SPACE CASE?

■ **A Make-Your-Own Alien Kit.**
Create your own fantastic forms of extraterrestrial life with this cool set of alien parts! Piece your way to page 20 to put 'em all together!

■ ***Greetings from Earth* CD.**
Hear the sounds that aliens might listen to someday! Rock on over to page 39 to start a cosmic jam session!

## THE SPACE UNIVERSITY WEB SITE

No cadet's quest for alien beings would be complete without this month's episode on the Space U web site. Make sure to visit the site to try out the Alien Assembly mission (where you can create even *more* aliens!). You can also test your skills at scanning the sky for alien radio signals!

Be sure to bring this month's password when you head for www.scholastic.com/space—because only Space U cadets with clearance will be allowed entry!

PLANET PASSWORD
This month's web site password is:
ALIENLIFE

Earn this month's mission patch by completing the games and challenges on the Space U web site. Then paste your patch right here!

Before you can find life in the universe, cadet, it helps to know what you're looking for. Try taking this quick quiz to see how much you know about life here on Earth:

On Earth, life...

**A.** Is a bowl o' cherries.

**B.** Is spelled "efil" backwards.

**C.** Requires the presence of these two things:
1) liquid water and 2) energy.

If you answered A, you've got a great outlook on life, and if you answered B, you're a stellar speller...but if you answered C, then you're really thinking like a Space U cadet!

As you might have heard, life can get pretty complicated—especially when you're trying to describe what it is. Here's a quick definition of life to get you started:

- A living creature contains all of the information (the recipe) needed to reproduce itself.

- It takes energy from its environment (in other words, it eats or absorbs stuff!).

- It grows, changes, and adapts to its surroundings.

Got it? Good! You're ready for more life lessons!

This is a model of a strand of DNA, which is found inside the cells of living things here on Earth. DNA contains the recipe for life—that is, the information that living things need to function, grow, and reproduce. So, whether you're a pumpkin, a mosquito, or a Space U cadet, your DNA will determine what you look like and what goes on inside you.

Like everything else in the universe, DNA is made up of atoms, and this model shows you the kinds of atoms that form DNA. The green balls represent carbon atoms (turn the page for more on the importance of carbon in our world!). The other colors represent oxygen, hydrogen, nitrogen, and phosphorus atoms.

# What Does Life Need?

**O**n Earth, all life uses carbon molecules as building blocks. What's carbon? It's an *element* (like oxygen and hydrogen) that's found in lots of different things, like the tip of your pencil, charcoal, and even diamonds!

Think of carbon as the "clinging friend"...once it grabs onto other elements, it hangs on tight—and forms molecules. These are called "organic" molecules, and they're the foundation of life on our planet.

What *else* does life need? Just two simple things:

**To join together, organic molecules need water.** In a dry environment, carbon molecules would just hang out by themselves. But add water—and BAM! A chemical reaction brings them together!

> **A** **molecule** is the smallest particle of a substance that has all the properties of that substance. A molecule is made up of one or more **atoms**.

**Life needs energy.** Here on Earth, that big shiny thing up in the sky (AKA the Sun) provides most of this. All the energy you get from the food you eat can be traced back to the Sun. We *used* to think that *all* life needed the Sun, but then we discovered creatures that live in complete darkness at the bottom of the ocean, thriving on heat energy from the Earth's core. (To meet them, turn to page 15!)

Now you know the story of life on Earth...but remember that life on other planets might be something completely different! Some scientists think that instead of carbon, aliens might be able to use silicon—an element that's found in sand (and computer chips!)—as the basic building block of life. And, in an alien world, energy might not be provided by a nearby star, but by underwater volcanoes, or even by the pull of gravity (see the Quick Blast below)!

## QuickBlast

### Feel the Heat!

**H**ow can the effects of gravity create energy? Grab a rubber band to find out!

**1** Stretch out the rubber band a few times.

**2** Quickly touch the rubber band to your chin. Do you feel warmth? That heat is the energy you created when you pulled the rubber band back and forth!

Now imagine that gravity is doing what you just did, pulling on something as huge as a moon or a planet. The heat from that interaction would be much more powerful, right? Well, that energy might be enough to support life (see page 17)!

# CREATE YOUR OWN LIFE DETECTOR!

> Cadet, turn back two pages if you missed out on the definition of life, an important clue in your hunt for aliens! But *knowing* what life is and *finding* it are two different things. Unfortunately, an ET probably won't walk up to you, stick out its hand (or sucker or claw) and say, "Hi, Space U cadet. I'm life." You really have to look for it!

## Launch Objective

> Detect signs of life!

## Your equipment

- 3 tall glasses
- 3 labels for the glasses
- 2 teaspoons salt
- 2 teaspoons yeast
- 2 teaspoons baking soda
- Pitcher
- 2 teaspoons lemon juice
- $\frac{1}{4}$ cup sugar
- 2 cups warm water

## Mission Procedure

**1** Label the glasses A, B, and C.

**2** Add the salt to glass A, the yeast to glass B, and the baking soda to glass C.

**3** Mix the sugar, the lemon juice, and the warm water in the pitcher.

**4** Pour equal amounts of the water mixture into each of the glasses.

**5** Things will start happening right away—but give your experiment 20 minutes to provide you with complete results. Where do you see signs of life?

## Science, Please!

Glass B and glass C got all bubbly, but glass A just sat there, right? Did you notice that glass C stopped bubbling after a short time, but glass B kept getting more and more bubbly? Way to go, cadet! You discovered signs of life!

That's right—the yeast in glass B is *alive*, and when you added the lemon-sugar water, the yeast started to chow down on the sugar. Things got bubbly, and the foam in the glass rose because the yeast's feeding process produced carbon dioxide gas.

Glass C *also* got bubbly, but not because baking soda is alive. What happened in glass C was a *chemical* reaction. When you added the water mixture, the baking soda reacted with it, and carbon dioxide gas was produced. (The lemon juice helped speed up the reaction between the baking soda and the water.) Once the baking soda finished reacting with the water, the bubbling stopped. The living yeast, on the other hand, continued to multiply and eat, creating more and more carbon dioxide bubbles.

The salt in glass A had no chemical reaction to the water mixture, so you didn't see any bubbles there. (Boring!)

## More from Mission Control

Try this mission again, but put the ingredients inside three separate plastic bags with zip closures. As soon as you've poured in the water mixture, seal the bags up and watch what happens. Which bag puffs up right away? After half an hour, which bag is the puffiest?

Once again, you can see how the live yeast keeps producing more and more gas as it eats and multiplies, while the baking soda's chemical reaction is over quickly.

## ✴Astrotales

### Life on Mars?

Is there life on Mars? In 1976, the world held its breath, waiting for the answer to that question. Two *Viking* spacecraft had just arrived on Mars and were about to start their life-detecting experiments.

As part of their testing, The *Viking* landers released nutrients into the Martian soil. Why? Just like when you added sugar to your glasses in this mission, the way the nutrients reacted with the soil would tell scientists back home whether the planet was lifeless or not.

Unfortunately for those hoping to hang out with Martians, *Viking* discovered that the Red Planet is kind of like glass C from this mission. After adding liquid and nutrients to the soil, the probes detected reactions, but NASA concluded that these were the result of non-living chemicals.

Of course, this doesn't mean that there's *definitely* no life on Mars. There may be evidence of life that's just waiting to be discovered...maybe by you!

# CREATE YOUR OWN L1FE DETECTOR!

# MOLD ON HOLD

> Don't look now, cadet, but you're surrounded! Countless mini-creatures are swirling in the air around you and even crawling on your skin! These microbes are all part of life on Earth, and many scientists think we'll find them elsewhere in the universe, too...*if we can detect them!*

## Launch Objective

> Show that microbes are all around us—even though we don't always notice them!

## Your equipment

> 2 slices of bread
> 2 plastic bags with zip closures
> Water
> Freezer

## Mission Procedure

**1** Sprinkle water on both slices of bread. Don't try to drench the slices—just make them moist.

**2** Put each slice in a plastic bag and seal it shut.

**3** Place one bag in the freezer and the other in a warm spot (like in a kitchen drawer).

**4** Check on the slices once a day for about ten days.

**5** You should notice mold growing on the bread in the warm spot. What's growing on the icy piece of bread? Nothing you can see!

## Science, Please!

What's one of the basic requirements of life on Earth, cadet? Liquid water. Sure, you sprinkled both slices of bread with water—but on the slice you popped in the freezer, the water turned to ice. The mold on the freezer bread couldn't use the solid form of water to multiply. The freezer's chilly temperature slowed down the microbes' growth anyway—if it didn't kill them altogether.

Back in the warm kitchen drawer, the life of microbes was much more pleasant. They had liquid water and warmth to help them multiply—and microbes grow at top speed in warm, moist environments. Mold can grow on bread by using the moisture that's already there, but by adding more water, you helped the mold grow even faster.

Where did the microbes come from in the first place? Did you sprinkle the bread with microbe powder or dip it in microbe sauce? We didn't think so. The microbes come from the air, which is filled with countless microbes. So, as you probe the universe for signs of life, don't be too quick to say a planet is lifeless—it might be filled with creatures that just need a closer look!

# Micro Marvels!

The world is full of weird creatures that are smaller than the eye can see. Some of them live in places you'd never expect! See if you can match each description with the right picture. You can check your answers on page 48.

**1 Dust mite:** About one million live in the average bed.

**2 Spirochete bacteria:** Live in sewage sludge.

**3 Tardigrade:** This "water bear" can live for years without food or water.

**4 Halobacteria:** These bacteria live in water four times saltier than sea water and can survive for years in dry salt crystals.

**5 Eyelash mites:** You guessed it...they live on human eyelashes (everyone's!).

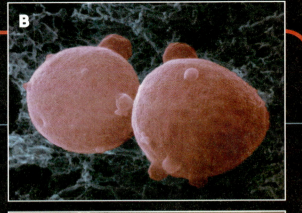

B

C

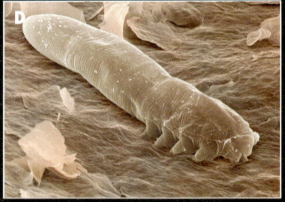

D

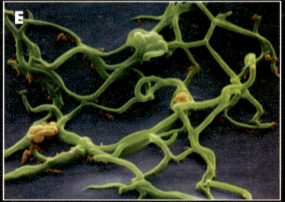

E

A

# THE "X" FILES

Are you ready to go to extremes?

Can you survive without ever seeing sunlight your entire life, thrive forever in near-boiling hot water, or stay trapped in almost solid rock for all of your days? If you answered "yes" to any of these questions, you might want to rethink calling yourself "human," and you might also have what it takes to be an *extremophile*.

Extremophiles are creatures who love extremes—extreme heat, extreme cold, extreme dryness, extreme everything! What might kill most other creatures is no problem for these weird wonders. What does all this have to do with the hunt for alien life in the universe? Lots! By studying these bizarre environments on Earth, scientists have the opportunity to research strange, alien places without ever having to leave our planet!

Here are just a few examples of extremophile environments:

■ Pools of hot sulfuric acid that would burn human skin or even melt metal are homes to heat-loving bacteria in Yellowstone National Park.

■ Solid rock over half a mile beneath the Earth's surface makes a cozy residence for this "rock-eating" bacteria.

■ Dry, sun-baked boulders in the desert are home to bacteria that create "desert varnish," which looks like a thin coat of black paint.

■ In the permanent ice and snow of Antarctica, a certain kind of algae can color entire snow banks red, orange, or green.

■ The deep, dark ocean floor is home to tube worms and other strange creatures—check out the next page for more on this!

## COULD THERE BE MICROBES ON THE MOON?

Maybe! Believe it or not, it's possible that some bacteria could still be alive in the human waste and food scraps left on the Moon by the six *Apollo* missions.

Sure, it's been three decades—not to mention the microbes would have to survive with no protection from massive heat, bitter cold, or harsh radiation. But there's a good chance that tough bacteria could overcome these conditions and reproduce inside small, damp spaces.

If they're reproducing, that means that bacteria have been born on the Moon that have never been to Earth—making them true ETs. So our nearest space neighbors could be closer than we thought! And if life has a chance on the Moon, who knows where else in the universe it might exist!

## QuickBlast

### Brush Up on Your Microbes!

Want to visit the home of some weird and wild microbes here on Earth? Here's how to find it:

1 Walk into the nearest bathroom.

2 Look in the mirror.

3 Open your mouth—and you're there!

That's right, cadet, your warm, wet mouth is a place where billions of microbes make a cozy home. Scientists have found hundreds of different species of bacteria living there! Who knows—some warm, wet planet across the universe could host a big, happy community of microbes a lot like yours!

# WHERE THERE'S SMOKE...

Cadet, until more space probes reach extreme habitats out in the universe, it's good practice to study the ones right here on Earth. And you'd have a tough time finding a more extreme habitat than the one created by the undersea BLACK SMOKER!

The first black smoker was discovered accidentally in 1977 by a research team. Where? On the ocean floor, 1.5 miles (2.4 km) below the Pacific Ocean's surface! The scientists discovered cracks and vents in the ocean floor that were gushing out jet-black, mineral-rich water ("black smoke"). As the scientists' underwater craft got closer to the black smokers, their temperature gauge started to melt—so they backed away. The water around these billowing chimneys can reach 662 degrees F (350 degrees C)!

Of course, nothing could live at temperatures this high, but creatures manage to get pretty close. There is a thin "life zone" between where the water is super hot and icy cold. Here, Earth's most heat-resistant bacteria live, able to survive in temperatures of 235 degrees F (113 degrees C).

Creatures like tube worms thrive around sea floor black smokers, growing up to 10 feet long (3 m). These worms actually never "eat" and have no digestive system. How do they survive? Millions of bacteria live inside their bodies, producing food that nourishes them.

Sunlight can't reach these deep black smokers...so how can life survive without energy from a star? The heat energy shooting up through the black smoker is an alternate energy source. This discovery helped open our minds to possible energy sources for life on other planets!

# UP IN

## Launch Objective

Create your own black smoker!

## Your equipment

- Piece of string about 2 feet (60 cm) long
- Baby food jar
- Food coloring (try using red and green to make a near-black color)
- Hot and cold water
- Large glass pitcher or vase (big enough for the jar to fit inside)

## Mission Procedure

**1** Tie one end of the string tightly around the mouth of the baby food jar. Then tie the other end of the string to the opposite side of the jar, creating a handle that you'll use in just a second.

**2** Fill up $\frac{3}{4}$ of the pitcher with cold water.

**3** Put a few drops of food coloring in the jar, then fill it to the top with hot tap water.

**4** Now the handle comes into action! Hold the jar by its "handle" and lower it gently into the pitcher.

**5** The colored water will rise up out of the jar—just like the hot mineral water from an erupting black smoker!

# SMOKE!

Because hot water rises in colder water, the colored hot water in your jar rushed up through the cold water. A black smoker works the same way—the water coming from under the ocean floor is so hot that it shoots up through the vent, rising quickly through the very cold water around it.

A black smoker on the ocean floor

## Life on Europa?

What do black smokers at the bottom of the ocean have to do with the hunt for aliens? Maybe quite a bit! The black smokers' environment may resemble conditions on Jupiter's moon Europa.

The *Galileo* space probe, which arrived at Jupiter in 1995, sent back images that allowed us to study Europa up close.

Based on information provided by *Galileo*, we know that Europa is covered by a layer of cracked ice. Beneath that ice there might be a liquid ocean that's heated by the constant pulling from nearby Jupiter (remember the Quick Blast from page 8?). Researchers believe that aquatic life might be able to live in some of the warmer areas of this ocean! But we won't know for sure until we get beneath the surface!

An up-close view of Europa, one of Jupiter's many moons

# ASTRO BIOLOGY

W hat is astrobiology? Well, like it sounds, it's a combination of astronomy and biology...but also geology and chemistry and much, much more! Astrobiologists explore questions like:

- Did life on Earth start in extreme environments (like black smokers), and is this how it might start on other planets?

- Can a planet recover from a worldwide disaster—like a giant asteroid smacking into it?

- How many planets could there be in the universe, and which ones could support life?

- Will our bodies be able to handle long periods in space as we travel to other worlds?

- Can we adapt to conditions in extraterrestrial environments once we get there?

- And why are humans so interested in searching for alien life forms anyway?

To make a long answer short, astrobiologists try to understand how the universe works and the way that living creatures fit into it all. (Phew!)

## ASTROBIOLOGIST
## Dr. Lynn Rothschild

Cadet, meet Dr. Lynn Rothschild, a real-life astrobiologist! Dr. Rothschild works in her lab at NASA's Ames Research Center in California to test how cells grow under various harsh conditions.

Dr. Rothschild also does field work in places like the hot springs of Yellowstone National Park (pictured here) to see if the results she gets in the lab match up with what organisms are really doing in nature.

**Question:** When did you know you wanted to be an astrobiologist?

**Answer:** When I was eight years old, I looked through a microscope and decided I wanted to study protists (organisms that have only one cell) and become a biologist.

**Q:** What's astrobiology all about?

**A:** Astrobiology is all about life! We focus on three questions: Where did life come from? Where is life going? And, are we alone in the universe? Most of our projects center on the question of how organisms, particularly microscopic ones, can survive in the natural environment.

**Q:** Can Earth microbes survive in space?

**A:** We know that some bacterial spores have survived on the outside of unmanned satellites. We're hoping to test a lot more species in the next five years. We want to put microbes outside the space station to see if they can survive.

**Q:** Have we been visited by aliens?

**A:** Probably, but not by little green men. They were probably microbes that came on meteorites that hit Earth. At one time, Mars might have been wet enough to sustain life. Something might have hopped aboard a rock before it got knocked off Mars by a meteorite impact. The rock could have flown off into space and crashed into Earth!

**Q:** Should we expect intelligent aliens to visit us?

**A:** If other intelligent life uses the same building blocks as we do, that means that they can only live so long. Aliens who wanted to make the long trip to Earth would have to go into hibernation or go through several generations to make the trip. Or aliens might explore the universe by sending out robots. If you think about it, that's exactly what we do—we send out unmanned exploration vehicles like the *Voyager* space probes, which are now beyond our solar system.

**Q:** What are the odds that aliens exist?

**A:** That's what the Drake equation tells us. (See page 32!) I think the odds are about 90 percent that there are aliens in the form of tiny microbes.

**Q:** What's in astrobiology's future?

**A:** Tons of things! For example, the Sun has about five billion years left in its lifetime. Astrobiologists can help think of something in the next few billion years, like resetting the Sun or moving the Earth! Or maybe the aliens we encounter will invite us over to their place!

## "Congrats! It's a Bouncing Baby Two-Headed Juhushuz!"

The Big Brains at Space U have an old saying: "Can't meet 'em? Make 'em!" What does *that* mean? It means that your next mission is to actually CREATE aliens!

This, of course, is something that would be impossible without the special items just waiting to be discovered in this month's Space Case.

This page shows what you'll find in your Make-Your-Own Alien kit. Use these parts to make whatever aliens you can imagine.

How do you put the aliens together? The answer is simple: However you want! A head can be a leg and a leg can be a body—whatever! Just insert the *plug* of one alien part into the *opening* on another part—and BAM! You're cooking up aliens!

Want to discover an added bonus feature of the light-colored alien parts? Click off the lights—they glow in the dark!

Glows in the dark!

Glows in the dark!

Glows in the dark!

Glows in the dark!

# THE STELLAR
## SIX-PLANET TOUR

To help you start creating your aliens, Space U has designed the **STELLAR SIX-PLANET TOUR**. As you turn the next few pages, you'll be transported to six different imaginary worlds scattered across the universe. It's up to you to investigate the environment and build an alien that could survive under these conditions!

Here are the stops on the **STELLAR SIX-PLANET TOUR**:

**1** PLANET **MACHISIMUS**
(Lots of gravity here!)

**2** PLANET **GLUBINSPLOOSH**
(Water, water, everywhere!)

**3** PLANET **AIRUPTHERE**
(*Air* you ready for air?)

**4** PLANET **PTHURST**
(Not a drop to drink...)

**5** PLANET **HOTSTUFF**
(Get fired up!)

**6** PLANET **SEEROGEE**
(Just "weight" a little!)

# Planet MACHISIMUS

**D**on't worry, it's not that triple deluxe cheeseburger you ate on the trip here that's making you feel so heavy. This planet has extremely high gravity—three times that of Earth's gravity! That means if you weigh 100 pounds (45 kg) on Earth, you now weigh 300 pounds (135 kg) on Machisimus. So, during your visit, you're going to feel a bit *squashed*. Hopefully you've been exercising to build up your muscles, because you'll need a lot of strength to walk or even raise your arms.

Did you remember your steel umbrella? Good! Because the high gravity makes the raindrops hit really hard—and you'd better watch out when that hail starts coming down! Yikes!

# Planet GLUBINSPLOOSH

Looking for a planet that has it all? Then Glubinsploosh is for you! The surface of this bitterly cold planet is pure ice. But deep down below the surface, hot gases from the planet's core bring the water to near boiling. Ice on top and heat below—who could ask for anything more?

Visiting cadets don't want to miss Mt. Crystal Clear! It's the tallest mountain in this region of the universe (seven times the height of our Mt. Everest!). It's made of solid ice, formed by water shooting up through the planet's icy surface. As the water lands, it freezes instantly!

UNDERWATER VIEW

# Planet AIRUPTHERE

Feeling gassy? Welcome to what locals call the Air Planet! This world is cloaked in many different kinds of gases that hover over the planet's rock core. Make sure to visit the floating city of Dontlukdown, which is twice the size of New York City and glides 80 miles (129 km) over the planet's surface.

Hold onto your space helmet—fast-moving winds gust at up to 350 miles per hour (563 km/h). With stormy clouds everywhere, visitors will see a lightning flash about once every second!

# Planet PTHURST

Space U teaches all cadets at least one thing about this planet: "If you don't have $H_2O$, do not go!" The surface of this world is almost completely without water. With temperatures that reach 160 degrees F (71 degrees C) during the day and –30 degrees F (–34 degrees C) at night, and massive dust storms with gusting winds—this isn't the place to visit if you're a fan of room temperature!

If you're looking for water, you'll have to dig for it. Deep below the surface, visitors can discover rivers of running water, flowing through tunnels with walls that naturally fluoresce (give off their own light).

Back up on the surface, cadets will want to check out "Mount Rage," a towering volcano. Fortunately it's no longer active, because it used to really blow its top!

UNDERGROUND VIEW

# Planet HOTSTUFF

Those cadets who like to hang out in hot spots have found the perfect place! This "fire planet" resembles early Earth, when it was still forming and was mostly melted rock. Also called the "lava planet," Hotstuff is covered by volcanoes that spew flames and rivers of fire. Thick smoke and high winds can make the air tough to breathe—so be sure to pack your oxygen tank!

A word of caution: Don't bother eating at the Ash & Dash. Even though it's one of Hotstuff's most legendary restaurants, Earthling visitors will not dine happily there. Their specialty is a carbon ash casserole that you would find about as appealing as a peanut-butter-and-squid taco!

# Planet SEEROGEE

This planet has very little gravity—and that means stuff here can almost float. Of course, this makes Seerogee a popular tourist spot for those who want to "lighten up" and feel freer. But Earthling visitors better bring their breathing equipment or they won't be feeling *anything*—because they won't live long. The low gravity means the planet can't hold on to gases like oxygen, and humans couldn't survive without special breathing gear.

As far as tourist hotspots go, be sure to check out Body Launcher Park! This amusement park has machines that can launch you high above the planet. Not to worry: The low gravity means you'll fall so slowly that the landing won't hurt.

# Life Is What You Make It!

Cadet, are there plenty of strange combinations in your alien creations? That's stellar! There is no right or wrong when it comes to making your aliens. Who's to say that creatures who inhabit the distant planets of the universe don't have springs for heads and heads for legs? Your imagination makes you just as qualified as anyone else to create alien masterpieces.

With that in mind, take a look at the ETs featured on this page. The aliens shown here represent just a few examples of the creatures that could have evolved to live in the conditions on each planet.

## Planet MACHISIMUS

Say hello to a **tuffster**! This alien's really got what it takes to stand up against the rough conditions on its planet. The extremely high gravity on Machisimus means that this creature has to be strong enough to resist the gravitational force that is constantly trying to pull it down. The tuffster also has tough skin that protects it from the sharp, stinging hail that can prove deadly to other creatures.

## Planet GLUBINSPLOOSH

Some think the **frigides** who live on the surface of this ice planet are kind of chilly. Actually they're very welcoming to visitors—when they're not busy skating or digging, that is. The frigides' pointy feet make wonderful skates that carry them easily over the planet's icy surface. These same feet can be used as ice picks to crack the frozen ground and dig for food that thrives in the warmer temperatures deep below the surface.

Shake fins with a **phlippian**! Also found on planet Glubinsploosh, this species swims in the dark waters below the icy surface. The thick ice overhead blocks out all light—so phlippians never see light from the nearest star. Instead, they survive on energy from the heat that shoots out through vents from inside the planet (like creatures that live around underwater black smokers back home on Earth). Gills located on their heads filter oxygen out of the water, and their little hair-like legs help them skitter along the sea floor.

## Planet AIRUPTHERE

Cadet, you'll really look up to the **flowter**! This species has adapted well to the gassy environment of the "air planet." They're able to easily expand and deflate their bodies as they inhale and release gases like helium. This means they can rise and descend like well-controlled hot air balloons. As they move through the air, their large mouths suck in hundreds of small insect-like creatures—talk about eating on the go!

## Planet PTHURST

The surface of the **littleliquids'** home world is all dried up—so these creatures live in tunnels beneath the surface where rivers of water still flow. The walls of these underground tunnels glow naturally, and littleliquids use their huge eyes with double pupils to capture as much of the dim light as they can. Their bodies also glow in the dark—which helps friends and family locate them in the dimmer parts of the tunnels!

## Planet HOTSTUFF

The **fireplugs** thrive in the raging fires of this lava planet. Their soft bodies are protected beneath their shell-like helmets. Just like turtles use their shells for protection, the fireplugs simply turn their helmets toward approaching flames and wait until the flames have died down. The wide mouths located underneath their bodies make it easy for the fireplugs to chow down on fallen ash (their favorite meal).

## Planet SEEROGEE

It helps to have a little spring in your step if you want to do well on this low-gravity planet—and that's exactly what the **coilers** have. Their springy legs allows these tall, thin creatures to jump extremely high. Coilers aren't just tall—they're also fast, and that's a good thing because the creatures they hunt are even faster!

# Part 3:
# Searching for Intelligent Life

Now that you've had a chance to imagine the kinds of alien creatures that might be out there, it's time to tackle the big question: If there is intelligent life elsewhere in the universe, how can we get in touch?

## ALL SETI!

Born in 1959, SETI (which stands for the "**S**earch for **E**xtra**T**errestrial **I**ntelligence") hunts for alien civilizations using radio telescopes that can detect radio waves coming from space. These big telescopes (like the ones you can see below) scan the sky for radio signals that an alien civilization might be broadcasting from a distant planet. Because radio waves travel really fast and far, we can receive them over great distances if our "ears" are tuned in and pointing in the right direction!

## LISTEN UP!

Just like it's hard for you to hear someone talk in a noisy cafeteria, SETI telescopes need peace and quiet to listen carefully. Thanks to more and more electronic "noise" from cell phones, radios, televisions, and other technology we use, time might be running out for SETI—at least on Earth. All the extra waves in the air could drown out signals that might be coming from extraterrestrials. What's the solution? SETI scientists have found a great spot on the far side of the Moon where they could build a lunar SETI base!

## RETI, SETI, GO!

Want to join in the hunt for extraterrestrial life? Then team up with an IGA (Intergalactic Adult) and visit the SETI@home web site at www.setiathome.ssl.berkeley.edu. SETI@home is an amazing project that lets millions of regular people be a part of the quest for ETs. Here's how it works: A special screensaver taps into the power of your computer when you're not using it—working to process the billions of pieces of data collected by the Arecibo radio telescope in Puerto Rico. Millions of people around the globe have signed up to be a part of the project!

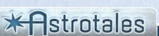

## *Astrotales

## Be Frank about ETs!

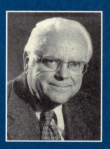

Frank Drake

American Frank Drake (born in 1930) was just eight years old when he started wondering about other beings in the universe. Later, he became an astronomer and was the first person to use radio telescopes to listen for signals from extraterrestrial life.

Drake developed a list of conditions that would have to occur for other intelligent life to exist out there.

■ There needs to be a galaxy where new stars are constantly being born.

■ There must be planets near one of the stars that could support life.

Life has to start on a planet.

■ The life has to evolve into intelligent creatures.

■ The intelligent creatures have to develop technology to communicate across the cosmos—but not destroy themselves with their own technology (like with nuclear war, for example).

This list forms the basis of a math equation (called the "Drake Equation") that scientists can use to estimate the chances that life exists elsewhere in the universe!

## SETI SCIENTIST
# Dr. Kent Cullers

Cadet, say hello to Dr. Kent Cullers—a leader in SETI's search for aliens!

Dr. Kent Cullers is a physicist, an astronomer, and the Director of SETI Research and Development. He also happens to be blind.

**Question:** Why did you get involved with SETI?

**Answer:** Because it was absolutely irresistible! I read the Cyclops Report, which proves that we could find a twin of our technology hundreds of thousands of light years away from Earth. I thought, "I want to be part of the search for a world like that!" I started with SETI in 1980 and have been there since.

**Q:** Does being blind affect your job?

**A:** I've been blind all my life. I was the first totally blind physicist and the first totally blind astronomer. I worked my way into radio astronomy—now I even do some visual astronomy. How do I do it? As with sighted people, everything these days is done on computer.

**Q:** Why is SETI so important to us?

**A:** Finding intelligent life will change our entire view of ourselves. To imagine creatures utterly different from us makes us realize how many things that we, as human beings, have in common and how valuable Earth is.

**Q:** Do you think we'll find aliens?

**A:** I am extremely hopeful that we will find intelligent life. It might not be easy or quick—the signal might be weak, and the universe is enormous. But there is a good chance we'll find it in the next fifty years. It could even be tomorrow!

**Q:** What are you looking for?

**A:** The natural universe makes complex and disorganized sounds. On the other hand, radio signals are produced from one source, and the waves are coordinated so they all run exactly in sync. We're looking for technology that is different from anything that nature can produce—that might lead us to an extraterrestrial civilization!

**Q:** What's next for SETI?

**A:** Things are going to get exciting because the search doubles in size every year and a half. So in fifty years, there will be a search a trillion times larger than what we have today!

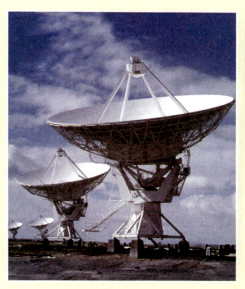

The Very Large Array, a group of radio telescopes in New Mexico

# WAVE HELLO!

**W**hile SETI listens and waits for radio waves from other planets, we're also making *lots* of waves ourselves.

Right now, as you read, the same radio and television waves that bring you music, news, cartoons, and commercials are speeding away from our planet in all directions. These waves travel at the speed of light, and they can reach far into space, even through the thick clouds of dust that prevent us from seeing distant stars. Already, our earliest radio and television signals are trillions of miles away!

So, does that mean aliens are sitting around watching our daytime soap operas? Probably not—not *yet* anyway. But each year, our TV and radio waves travel farther, making it more and more possible that some distant alien civilization might hear (and see!) us.

But if they *do* pick up our waves and send back a response, how long will it take for us to get the message? Try the Quick Blast below to get an idea!

## Hellooo?

**H**ow long would it take to exchange greetings with an ET? Suppose you wanted to chat with an ET on a planet in Proxima Centauri's solar system—which is 4.2 light years away. If you sent a "hello" message by radio, how long would you have to wait for a response from the ET?

**A)** 4.2 months    **B)** 4.2 years    **C)** 8.4 years

You can check your answer on page 48!

YOU: Knock knock.

ET: Who's there?

YOU: Space.

ET: Space who?

YOU: Not Space who. Space U!

(Transmission terminated by alien life form.)

# ALIEN MATH TEST

The Arecibo radio telescope

In 1974, a message was beamed into space from the Arecibo radio telescope in Puerto Rico. The message consisted of a long series of 1's and 0's, like this:

0000001010101000000000000101000001010000000100100010001000100010...

The whole message, all 1,679 digits of it, is now traveling across the universe. Someday it might be received by an alien civilization, and they'd better be ready with their pencils sharpened and their brains on turbo! Because those lucky aliens are supposed to use the 1's and 0's to create the picture below. How are they supposed to do that?

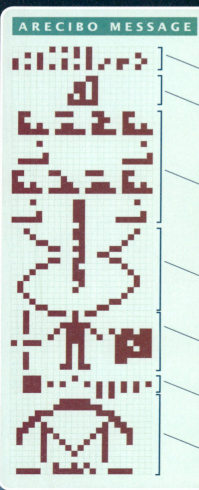

## ARECIBO MESSAGE

The numbers one through ten, to help the aliens understand how numbers will be represented throughout the message.

This area shows the five most important elements on Earth: hydrogen, carbon, nitrogen, oxygen, and phosphorus.

This is a breakdown of the substances that make up our DNA, the molecule in our cells that holds all the information human beings need to function and reproduce.

The spiral structure of our DNA.

An outline of a human being, with the world's population on the right and the human's height on the left.

Our solar system, with Earth above the other planets to highlight it.

A picture of the Arecibo radio telescope, to let the aliens know how we beamed them the message.

Well, to start, they'll have to realize that the number 1,679 is the result you get when you multiply 23 and 73. Those two numbers are special because they're prime numbers (numbers that can only be divided evenly by themselves and 1).

*Then* the aliens will have to figure out that they need to create a grid that's 73 rows tall and 23 columns wide. After that, these super-smarties will have to put the 1's and the 0's into the squares of the grid, shade in all the 1 squares, and leave the 0 squares blank. All done? Not quite. Now comes the fun part! They have to figure out the meaning of all the symbols in the picture on the left.

Do you think the aliens will get the message? Try the next mission to see how *you'd* do if *you* picked up a transmission like this!

# AL1EN CODE

01100000011011001101100000010010

## Launch Objective

▶ Decode an alien message!

## Your equipment

▶ Pencil

## Mission Procedure

### Part 1: First Contact

**1** Here's the alien's message:

```
0 1 0 1 0
0 1 0 1 0
0 1 1 1 0
0 1 0 1 0
0 1 0 1 0
0 0 0 0 0
0 1 1 1 0
0 1 0 0 0
0 1 1 0 0
0 1 0 0 0
0 1 1 1 0
0 0 0 0 0
0 1 0 0 0
0 1 0 0 0
0 1 0 0 0
0 1 0 0 0
0 1 1 1 0
0 0 0 0 0
0 1 0 0 0
0 1 0 0 0
0 1 0 0 0
0 1 0 0 0
0 1 1 1 0
0 0 0 0 0
0 1 1 0 0
1 0 0 1 0
1 0 0 1 0
1 0 0 1 0
0 1 1 0 0
```

**2** Copy the message into the grid on the right, putting one digit in each box. Start at the top left corner and work your way across each row, from the top of the grid to the bottom.

**ET KEY**

| **1** | = BLACK |
| **0** | = WHITE |

**3** Using the ET key, fill in the squares of the grid.

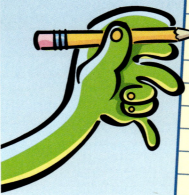

**4** Examine the grid to find the message! You can check your answer on page 48.

# Part 2: Code Challenge

Feeling confident? Take the code one step further! This time, you'll get the message the same way that aliens might someday receive the message that was beamed out from the Arecibo radio telescope in 1974 (see page 35). You'll have to figure out what size grid to use. Think you're up to the challenge?

**1** Here's the next message:

```
0 0 0 0 0 0 0 1 1 0 1 1 0 0 1 1 0 1 1
0 0 0 0 0 0 0 0 0 0 1 0 0 0 0 0 1 1
1 0 0 0 0 0 0 0 0 0 1 0 0 0 1 0 0 1 0
0 0 1 0 0 0 1 1 1 0 0 0 0 0 0 0 0 0
```

**2** Count all the digits in the message to get the total number. You can check your answer on page 48.

**3** What two prime numbers can you multiply together to get this total? (See page 35 for a review of prime numbers.) Again, you can check your answer on page 48.

**4** Now make your grid. The larger prime number tells you how many boxes *tall* your grid should be, and the smaller prime number indicates how many boxes *wide* it should be. Use the workspace below to make your grid.

**5** Copy the message into your grid, giving each digit its own box.

**6** Color in each box that has a 1. See the image? Smile! You did it!

## Science, Please!

This code isn't *really* so other-worldly—it's used on Earth all the time. It's the language that computers speak, called *binary code*.

Computers are kind of like light switches and can only tell the difference between "on" and "off." They translate these two positions into the numbers 1 and 0. By creating long series of 1's and 0's, computers are able to store, process, and present all sorts of information—like book reports, music, or video games. Pretty neat tricks for two simple numbers!

## More from Mission Control

Ready for more alien messages? Then visit this month's Space U web site (www.scholastic.com/space) and print out the Alien Code Log pages. They've got more alien codes for you to crack and the supplies you need to send alien transmissions to your friends!

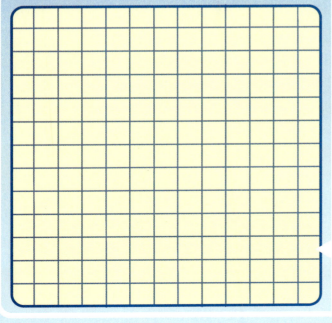

**CODE WORKSPACE**
To make your grid, just draw a box around the area you need. (If you're not sure how big your grid needs to be, check page 48!)

# FROM EARTH WITH LOVE!

Cadet, when you can't visit distant friends in person, isn't it always nice to send a card—or a super high-tech space probe? For years, we've been launching probes out into deep space. Here are just two examples:

## PIONEER

NASA sent a plaque carrying a message from Earth on the space probes *Pioneer 10* and *11*, which were launched in 1972 and 1973. The message was made up of pictures, including a man and woman, the planets of our solar system, and a map showing where our Sun is located in our galaxy.

A *Pioneer* space probe

Here's our solar system, as shown on the *Pioneer* plaque. You can see the path that *Pioneer* took on its way out of our solar system.

## VOYAGER

Two *Voyager* probes were launched in 1977, each with a gold-plated record full of sounds, greetings, and images from Earth. (See the next few pages for more on this!)

By 1990, both *Voyager* probes were beyond the orbit of Pluto and have since left our solar system. They're now the farthest man-made objects from Earth!

A *Voyager* space probe

The surface of *Voyager*'s Golden Record

# EARTH'S GREATEST HITS!

In this month's Space Case, you've got your very own mini-version of the Golden Record that's now riding aboard the *Voyager* space probes, way out in deep space.

The original Golden Record is not a CD like yours (since there were no CDs back in the 1970s when the *Voyager* probes were launched). Instead, it's the old-fashioned kind of record, about the size of a small pizza. It's covered in gold to keep it from getting battered or broken as it zooms through space.

If aliens ever find *Voyager*'s Golden Record, they'll have to be smart enough to figure out how to play it. To help the aliens along, the record's cover has lots of diagrams that show how the record works, and *Voyager* is carrying some of the parts the aliens will need to construct their record player.

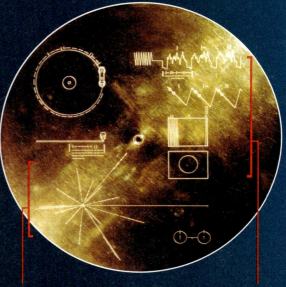

The cover of the Golden Record

This diagram shows the position of our Sun in relation to our galaxy's pulsars.

These diagrams show how to play the record.

If the aliens manage to play the record, here's what they'll find:

- **Greetings in fifty-five Earthling languages.** (Your CD has twenty-five of these greetings. Turn the page to find out what they mean!)

- **Sounds of Earth**, like crashing waves, rumbling thunder, howling dogs, crying babies, and roaring jets. (Your CD has all of these sounds—check out pages 42–43 for the full list!)

- **Music** from different cultures and time periods.

- **Images**, including photos of people and places on Earth.

Who decided what to put on the record? All the material was selected by a committee led by the famous astrophysicist Dr. Carl Sagan (remember him from your first month at Space U?). To meet another one of the record's creators, turn to page 44!

# Greetings
## FROM
## EARTH

As you listen to the greetings on your CD, look at these pages to find out where each language is spoken and what the greeting means. What do you imagine alien listeners will think when they hear all these different voices?

**Track 1. SUMERIAN**
May all be well. (This is an ancient language, spoken thousands of years ago in what is now Iraq.)

**Track 2. GREEK**
Greetings to you, whoever you are. We come in friendship to those who are friends.

**Track 3. CANTONESE**
Hi. How are you? We wish you peace, health, and happiness.

**Track 4. RUSSIAN**
Be healthy—I greet you.

**Track 5. THAI**
We in the world send you our goodwill.

**Track 6. ARABIC**
Greetings to our friends in the stars. We hope that we will meet you someday.

**Track 7. ROMANIAN**
Greetings to everybody.

**Track 8. SPANISH**
Hello and greetings to all.

**Track 9. KECHUA**
Greetings from Earth, in the Kechua language.

**Track 10. LATIN**
Greetings to you, whoever you are. We have goodwill toward you and bring peace across space.

**Track 11. DUTCH**
Heartfelt greetings to everyone.

**Track 12. URDU**
Peace to you. We the inhabitants of this Earth send our greetings to you.

**Track 13. VIETNAMESE**
We sincerely send you our friendly greetings.

**Track 14. JAPANESE**
Hello. How are you?

**Track 15. HINDI**
Greetings from the inhabitants of this world.

**Track 16. ITALIAN**
Many greetings and wishes.

**Track 17. NGUNI [ZULU]**
We greet you, great ones. We wish you a long life.

**Track 18. ARMENIAN**
To all those who exist in the universe, greetings.

**Track 19. NEPALI**
Wishing you a peaceful future from the Earthlings!

**Track 20. MANDARIN CHINESE**
Hope everyone's well. We are thinking about you all. Please come here to visit us when you have time.

**Track 21. NYANJA**
How are all you people of other planets?

- 25
- 8
- 9

Track **22. GUJARATI**
Greetings from a human being of the Earth. Please contact.

Track **23. PERSIAN**
Hello to the residents of far skies.

Track **24. CZECH**
Dear friends, we wish you the best.

Track **25. ENGLISH**
Hello from the children of planet Earth.

**QuickBlast**

## My Greeting to the Universe

What would *you* say if you could send a greeting to an ET across the universe? Write your message below:

_____

_____

_____

_____

# The SOUNDS of EARTH

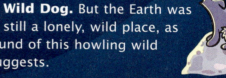

This part of the *Voyager* Golden Record is a collection of sounds that tell the story of Earth—from our planet's earliest days to modern times. As you listen, think about how an alien would imagine Earth after hearing all these sounds!

**TRACK 26** **Music of the Spheres.** This eerie music was created by mathematicians who calculated the orbits of the planets around the Sun and turned the numbers into sounds.

**TRACK 27** **Volcanoes, Earthquakes, and Thunder.** Young planet Earth had lots of volcanoes, earthquakes, and storms. This activity brought about the beginnings of life on Earth....

**TRACK 28** **Mud Pots.** Life probably began in giant bubbling puddles. These sounds are meant to bring to mind that environment.

**TRACK 29** **Wind, Rain, Surf.** For hundreds of millions of years, the Earth's own sounds were all that could be heard on our planet.

**TRACK 30** **Crickets and Frogs.** These critters' noises represent the first time living beings on Earth could make noise.

**TRACK 31** **Birds, Hyena, Elephant.** Life continued to evolve on Earth, and the animal kingdom grew.

**TRACK 32** **Chimpanzee.** The appearance of primates like monkeys and chimps marked the beginning of conscious life—the ancestors of humans!

**TRACK 33** **Wild Dog.** But the Earth was still a lonely, wild place, as the sound of this howling wild dog suggests.

**TRACK 34** **Footsteps, Heartbeats, Laughter.** These sounds represent the entrance of the first human beings.

**TRACK 35** **Fire and Speech.** Here you can hear a greeting in the !Kung language, spoken by African hunters and gatherers. The "!" stands for a click or pop of the tongue.

**TRACK 36** **The First Tools.** Thousands of years ago, early humans carved all their tools by chipping away at rocks.

**TRACK 37** **Tame Dog.** Before long, people learned to tame wild animals. This dog sounds much less scary than the howling wild dog you heard earlier.

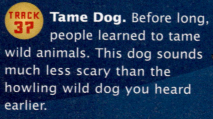

**Herding Sheep.** After people had learned to tame and raise animals, they could settle on farms instead of traveling around to hunt wild beasts.

 **Blacksmith Shop, Sawing.** As humans grew more advanced, they began making and building things with better tools.

 **Tractor and Riveter.** These strong pieces of machinery meant that people were able to build greater things than ever before. A riveter uses strong fasteners called rivets to attach two pieces of metal together.

 **Morse Code.** These beeps are Morse code for "Ad astra per aspera," which means "To the stars through difficulties" in Latin. Morse code uses short and long beeps to represent the letters of the alphabet.

 **Ships.** Sure, we can travel by spaceship these days, but there was a time when ships on the water were a big step in transportation.

 **Horse and Cart.** This horse and cart start out on a dirt road and end up on a paved road. Can you hear the difference?

**Train.** You can imagine how fast this train is moving by the way the sound seems to travel from one side of you to the other.

 **Truck, Tractor, Bus, Automobile.** In the past hundred years, the transportation we use has become faster and better.

**F-111 Jet Flyby.** You can hear the flying jet whizzing by one ear and then the other, just like you could with the train. But unlike the train, the F-111 can move faster than the speed of sound!

 **_Saturn 5_ Rocket Liftoff.** The _Apollo_ missions that took men to the Moon were each launched on a _Saturn 5_ rocket.

**Kiss.** You can recognize a kiss, but would aliens know what they were hearing?

**Mother and Child.** Here's a crying baby and the sounds of a mother comforting the child.

**Life Signs.** These sounds come from the recorded brainwaves, heartbeat, and eye and muscle movements of one of the record's creators, Ann Druyan (meet her on page 44!).

**Pulsar.** When scientists first heard these noises coming from space, they thought they could be a message from an ET. Now we know that these pulsating radio waves come from spinning stars called pulsars.

# Ann Druyan
## CREATIVE DIRECTOR OF THE VOYAGER GOLDEN RECORD

Meet Ann Druyan, one of the people who worked with astrophysicist Carl Sagan to create the *Voyager* Golden Record!

In addition to her work on the Golden Record, Ann Druyan has written and produced movies and TV shows about science and space.

Ms. Druyan is also the Program Director of *Cosmos 1*, the world's first solar sailing spacecraft mission (a solar sail is a spacecraft that's propelled by sunlight, like a sailboat is propelled by wind!).

**Question:** Who are the people who spoke the greetings on the Golden Record?

**Answer:** The greetings were recorded at a sound studio at Cornell University in Ithaca, New York. The speakers were students, professors, and other people from Cornell's community who could speak a language fluently. The seven-year-old boy who said "Hello from the children of planet Earth" was Carl Sagan's son, Nick.

**Q:** How did you choose the languages for the greetings?

**A:** We wanted to have greetings from the languages with the most living speakers on Earth, such as Mandarin Chinese and English. However, we also wanted to give a sense of how we communicated with each other a long time ago, so we included some ancient languages, like Sumerian, whose speakers all died out long ago.

**Q:** How did you decide which sounds to include in *The Sounds of Earth*?

**A:** I would walk around with my eyes closed trying to hear what life sounds like (without bumping into things). I made lists of every sound I could think of and then discussed them with Carl Sagan and the other people working on the record.

**Q:** Which was the hardest sound to collect?

**A:** The kiss. We tried everything, even arm-sucking, to get that smoochy sound. We wanted it to sound really good because this was to be a kiss that could last a billion years. After lots of people kissing each other, we finally got it right.

**Q:** Which is your favorite sound, and why?

**A:** My favorite sound is the tender voice of a mother talking to her newborn baby for the very first time. I often wonder who that little baby grew up to be and if he knows that the very first sounds he ever made are bound for interstellar space and a future that could be a billion years long.

**Q:** What kind of impression of Earth do you think aliens would get from *The Sounds of Earth*?

**A:** They'd hear that this little world is abuzz with life and activity. There's lots going on here. The Earth is home to a wondrous variety of life!

The surface of the *Voyager* Golden Record

# Part 4:
# Past Mysteries and Future Possibilities

## IS THAT AN ALIEN AT MY DOOR?

Some people believe that **UFO**s (Unidentified Flying Objects) have been visiting Earth for thousands of years. "UFO" is often used as just another word for an alien spaceship—but it also includes any light or object in the sky that can't be explained.

## THE HISTORY OF THE UFO MYSTERY

Reports of UFOs can be found throughout history. Here are just a few:

- **2345 B.C.**: In Chinese history, there is a record of "ten flying suns" appearing in the sky, scorching the Earth and killing trees and plants.

- **1600 B.C.**: In Egypt, legend has it that a circle of fire appeared in the sky over the palace of the Pharaoh. Lots of fish and winged creatures are said to have rained down as it flew away.

- **216 B.C.**: A Roman historian recorded that "things that looked like ships" were seen in the sky over Italy.

- **1561** and **1566**: In Germany, people claimed they saw colored rods and spheres flying around the sky for about an hour. Five years later, in Switzerland, people claimed that "large black globes" appeared in the sky.

"Large black globes" were seen in Switzerland in 1566.

- **1947**: An American pilot named Kenneth Arnold said he spotted nine objects—each longer than a whale and flying more than 1,200 miles per hour (1,931 km/h). He said that each moved like "a saucer would if you skipped it across water." Thanks to Kenneth and the news stories that followed, soon everyone was calling UFOs "flying saucers."

- **1952** to **1969**: The U.S. Air Force kept track of UFO sightings through "Project Blue Book." 12,318 sightings were recorded—most were explained, but 701 of the sightings are still a mystery!

## UFO? SORRY, NO

Contrary to what some Hollywood movies would have you think, a real flying saucer and actual evidence of an alien visit have never been discovered. It's true, cadet: Scientists have never pointed at something and said, "Yes, we know that is an alien spaceship."

Then how can we explain all the alien sightings through the centuries? Most were probably strange weather patterns or wild flashes caused by ball lightning (which can occur just after a thunderstorm and looks like a glowing ball of light). In the past 100 years, many sightings turned out to be weather balloons, test airplanes, or simple pranks pulled by people trying to get attention.

## ★ Astrotales

## Is All Well at Roswell?

In 1947, the wreckage of a crash was discovered in a field near Roswell, New Mexico. The U.S. Army sent out an investigator and released a statement reporting that a "flying disk" had been recovered. Within twenty-four hours, however, the Army sent out a "correction." There was no flying disk, they said, only bits and pieces of a plain old weather balloon that had crashed. But for decades, some people suspected that the government was covering something up, pointing to evidence that included the following:

The official photo of the Roswell wreckage

- The Army investigator who was involved in the "correction" later said that he had been made to pose with pieces of wreckage that were not recovered at the site.

- The person who discovered the crash was kept a virtual prisoner by the Army for a week and never spoke of the crash again.

- A secret flight left Roswell, carrying a mysterious crate (some think that dead aliens were inside the crate).

Finally, in 1993, the Army launched another investigation—and admitted there really *had* been a cover-up! The balloon that had crashed was actually an experimental *spy* balloon, not a weather balloon as they had originally said. But, they added, no aliens were ever present at Roswell. What do you think, cadet?

# MAYBE, SOMEDAY...

## MS. MANNERS'S GUIDE TO WELCOMING ALIENS TO EARTH

Cadet, imagine a shipload of aliens arriving on Earth, looking for a little Earthling hospitality on their way to a distant galaxy. Is there a global plan in place for how the planet should deal with the alien visitors? Who should represent Earth in conversations with the ETs?

These questions aren't as easy to answer as you might think. Remember that we often disagree with our neighbors on Earth, so it might be tricky for us to speak with one unified voice.

As of now, there's no global rulebook that would tell us what to do. Sure, SETI has a very loose plan in case of alien contact: Basically, tell the world about the contact and gather scientists together to decide on the next steps.

But the idea of alien contact seems so, well, *alien* to many people that it's hard to get them to take the idea seriously. So far, attempts by scientists to get the United Nations to come up with some kind of plan in case of alien contact have been met with silence or simple "no"s. It might be up to you, cadet, to create a worldwide plan for dealing with alien encounters!

## WHAT'S NEXT IN THE SEARCH FOR LIFE?

Before you put out your cosmic welcome mat, remember that the universe is a *really* huge place, so we're far more likely to make contact with other intelligent beings through radio signals across the distance. And what's next on that front?

Scientists have been working to improve the technology that helps us spot new planets beyond our solar system (these are called *exoplanets*—and you can learn all about them in another Space U book, *The Space Explorer's Guide to Planets, Moons, and More*!). Once we've identified new exoplanets, we can aim our telescopes toward them to see if we can pick up any promising signals. And that's exo-lent news for ET-seekers!

# Life
## Goes On!

Yes, cadet, you've come to the end of your training in the search for life in the universe...but that doesn't mean your quest should end!

Your imagination has lots to work with, now that you've checked out some of the weird creatures that share your planet and concocted a few alien creations of your own. Keep on imagining the different forms your cosmic neighbors might take, and keep thinking about the variety of places where they could live. Who knows, maybe you could be the first to find them!

And if you manage to find *intelligent* life beyond Earth, will you know how to make contact? Put your cosmic communication skills to one final test with the message on the right. (If you didn't learn the Alien Code on pages 36–37, now's your chance!) Check your answer below, and we'll see ya next month!

### THE ANSWER STATION

- Page 12: **Micro Marvels!**
  1) A   2) E   3) C   4) B   5) D

- Page 34: **Hellooo?**
  C) 8.4 years. (Your "hello" would take 4.2 years to reach the ET, and the ET's response would take another 4.2 years to reach you.)

- Page 36: **Alien Code**
  Part 1: The message says "Hello."
  Part 2: 2) The total number is 77.
  3) 7 X 11  = 77
  4) The grid should be 11 boxes tall and 7 boxes wide.
  6) The image is a smiley face.

- Page 48: **Life Goes On**
  The message says "See ya."